Puberty Survival Guide
for Girls

Puberty Survival Guide for Girls

Written by Dr. Eve Anne Ashby with illustrations by Dr. Richard Stewart

iUniverse, Inc.

New York Lincoln Shanghai

Puberty Survival Guide for Girls

Copyright © 2005 by Eve Anne Ashby

iUniverse books may be ordered through booksellers or by contacting:

iUniverse
2021 Pine Lake Road, Suite 100
Lincoln, NE 68512
www.iuniverse.com
1-800-Authors (1-800-288-4677)

ISBN-13: 978-0-595-34220-4 (pbk)
ISBN-13: 978-0-595-78990-0 (ebk)
ISBN-10: 0-595-34220-5 (pbk)
ISBN-10: 0-595-78990-0 (ebk)

Printed in the United States of America

Contents

Welcome to one of the most important times of your life-PUBERTY! This is a special time when you will grow into an adult. *Everything* will change from your nose to your toes! Your brain will start working in more complex ways. Your skin and hair will change. Your female hormones will start kicking in making your body look more like a woman and less like a child.

It will take many years to complete this transformation. You may *think* that you're not changing at all but you are! When you're 16, you may look at your 5th grade picture and be pretty amazed how your journey through puberty has changed everything about you. The human brain is amazing; it has a schedule for all of these changes mapped out specifically for YOU. Your body will start this exciting time of change as a girl and finish as a woman capable of doing the most amazing things!

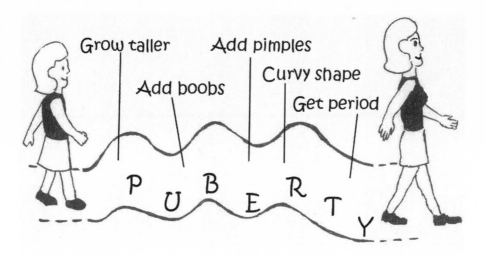

So why do I need to know about puberty if it's going to happen anyway?

One day you'll buy your first car and with that car you'll receive an owner's manual. The owner's manual will tell you how to take care of your car. Think of this guide as an owner's manual for your body. In it you will learn why your body is going these changes and how to deal with them. There is a reason for every change that you will experience. By understanding your body, you will be able to take care of it for the rest of your life.

As a gynecologist (a doctor that just takes care of women), I have met many women who are confused about their own bodies. I'm here to set the record straight. If anything you read is hard to understand or different from what you were taught, ask your mom, school nurse or other close friend to clear things up for you. If you are still confused then ask your doctor at your next checkup.

Your body goes through some pretty cool changes during puberty. Some of these changes will make you happy; some will make you not so happy. Many girls look forward to growing taller and becoming more mature; on the other hand, many girls may not be looking forward to having acne or getting their period.

As your brain matures and you start to think more like an adult, you will be given more responsibility and be allowed more independence from your parents. As you go through puberty, you will gain confidence in yourself. This confidence will make you proud of the woman that you are becoming.

How long will puberty take?

Puberty usually starts between the ages of 8 and 13. It will end when you reach your adult height and weight. This is usually around age 16 or 17. Every human being goes through puberty-even the boys! The difference is that the changes of puberty happen at different times and in different ways for different people. For example, a boy may grow taller at the *end* of puberty and for many girls this is often one of the first changes to happen.

There are some very distinct differences that will separate the boys from the girls during this time. Girls will develop breasts and will start their periods. Boys will grown thick facial hair and become more muscular. Girls will start to develop a curvy figure and a boy's voice will deepen and sound more like a man. Girls' voices get deeper as well, but not as drastically.

All of these changes are on a specific time schedule stored in your brain. Your brain guides all of these changes by using chemical messengers called *hormones*. Hormones affect many different parts of your body. They act on tissues that will develop into breasts, help bones to grow taller and stronger, help develop muscles, and will help develop your internal female organs. These chemical messengers also work on your thoughts and emotions and will affect everything you say and do. Hormones need proper vitamins and nutrients found in a healthy diet and body fat to work.

Sometimes it may feel a little bit overwhelming to know that you're going through so many changes. Don't worry, things happen slowly enough to let you become comfortable with your body along the way.

For girls, many changes overlap each other. Major things may become noticeable within a year or it may take a few years. During this time the shape of your body will change, breasts will begin to develop, your waist will become smaller and your hips a little wider. Your changing shape will make you look more like a woman and less like a little girl. Your skin will start to secrete more oils that will make you feel and smell differently. Most importantly, your female organs will grow and start to function as a woman and you'll get your period.

When is this going to happen to me?

Everyone's body is different and we all have different time clocks. When you were in kindergarten, everyone didn't learn the alphabet at the same time but by the time 1st grade rolled around everyone knew it backward and forward. This is the same sort of thing that happens with puberty. Some girls may start the early changes of puberty around age 7; but most start a few years later. You may start puberty the same time as your mother or other female relatives in your family did. You might want to ask your mother how old she was when she started developing or started getting her period. Since this subject is pretty personal, I would wait to ask her when you are alone together instead of at dinner with the whole family!

The beginning of puberty also has a lot to do with the food you eat, your weight, and even where you live. Girls with unhealthy diets may start puberty at an older age then those with good eating habits; girls who have extra weight may start to develop sooner than thinner girls. Some girls living on higher elevations (like in the mountains of Colorado) may start their journey to womanhood later then girls who live near sea level (like the East Coast). African-American girls usually start puberty around 8 or 9 while lighter skinned girls start a little bit later around age 10.

You may notice that some girls in your class have already started to develop breasts and even had a period before anything has happened to you. *This is OK.* Again, your body is doing what is right for you and eventually you will all catch up with each other. If you reach 15 or 16 and haven't started to develop at all then you may need a visit to the doctor to check on your time clock.

Are all of these changes going to happen at once?

Even though many of the changes of puberty overlap each other, I've tried to separate them to help you understand what's happening to different parts of your body. To make things easier, I've divided the major changes you'll notice into four categories: growth spurt, breast changes, skin and hair changes, and finally, getting your period. Usually girls go through a growth spurt at the start of puberty and then develop breasts and pubic hair. Getting your menstrual cycle is usually at the end of puberty but you may still continue to grow after that. Changes in your skin and hair will continue into adulthood but may not be as noticeable as when you were going through adolescence.

As you mature into an adult, there are many other changes going on in your brain, heart, lungs, and the rest of your internal organs. Although the most noticeable changes are on the outside, it's important to remember that your whole body grows and matures in many ways. This is why it's important to nourish your body with healthy foods and exercise to help keep you well. By having healthy habits, you'll be able to keep up with the changes going on inside as well as outside.

GROWTH SPURT

"I just bought these shoes 3 months ago and now they're too tight!"
(Laura, age 10)
"I'm the shortest girl in my class, will I ever be tall?" (Annie, age 12)
"Am I too fat?" (Cherise, age 9)
"I'm taller than all the boys in my class, am I a freak?" (Casey, age 12)

Many girls notice the outside changes happening to their body as one of the first signs of puberty. Most girls start sprouting up around age 10. This is usually the first clue that your puberty time clock is working. You will notice that you're growing out of your shoes pretty fast or your pants are shorter on you then when you bought them. Your friends and family members who haven't seen you for a few months might notice that you've grown taller. You may notice that your clothes are a little tighter or you need to take a larger size than you did last season.

You've actually had a few other growth spurts before this one but mainly when you were a baby. This one takes a little longer and will be your final one. It will end when you are an adult. Not only will you be growing taller, you will be gaining weight as well. This is normal and is necessary to develop into a healthy adult. School nurses and your doctor will usually keep a chart of your height and weight at each visit to make sure that you are growing on schedule.

How tall will I be as an adult?

Before puberty, you grew about 2 inches a year. Once your growth spurt hits you may spring up almost 4 inches in a year! Your height rapidly increases over 3 or 4 years and will start to slow down once you start your menstrual cycle. Most girls reach their adult height within 3 years of their first period. Your adult height is usually about the same as your parent's heights. How tall you were before your growth spurt is also a good esti-mate of your adult height. If you were short as a child as compared to oth-ers in your class you may be short as an adult. No rule is perfect; the shortest girl in your first grade class may be the tallest girl in your 8^(th) grade class.

In order to grow taller, the bones in your body and legs need to grow longer and thicker. Many times your feet will be the first to change. You might find you're growing out of your shoes before they're even broken in! Some girls may feel proud that their feet are growing so fast (they may even be able to fit in mom's high heels!). Other girls may be embarrassed by their big feet. Just remember that the rest of your body will grow and catch up and everything will be in the right proportion when you've com-pleted puberty.

The most important thing to know about this time of growing taller is that what you eat now will determine how strong your bones will be for the *rest of your lifetime*. If you eat foods with a lot of calcium like milk, cheese, yogurt, and those in a green salad you will have very strong bones as an adult. This is so important because you won't be able to make such strong bones when you are an adult. You'll be happy you fed your body these good things when you get older because your bones will continue to be strong. Try not to drink too many soft drinks because this may lead to very weak and brittle bones when you are an adult. Instead, drink a few glasses of milk a day and eat cheese, salad and plenty of vegetables.

Exercise now will also help your bones later. When you exercise, like running, bicycling, and swimming, you are helping the inside of your bones to become stronger and develop better. Make sure you are exercising at least 30 minutes a day. As you get older, your bones may lose this strength if you don't keep up these healthy habits. In some older women, their bones become so weak that they become shorter and hunched over. By getting involved in sports, walking, and eating well *now,* you will make sure that you will be healthier when you are an adult.

Boys usually go through their growth spurt later than girls. Boys grow taller and more muscular around their upper body starting around age 12 or 13. This is why 11 and 12-year-old boys are often shorter then girls their age. So, girls, 6th grade is a good time to challenge the boys to a basketball game Good luck!

How much will I weigh when I finish puberty?

To balance out your increasing height you may notice that you are getting a little heavier. This is *normal*. You may gain 10–15 pounds in just one year. You might notice that some extra weight goes from being around your waist to around your hips or even to your breasts! This is because your brain is growing and releasing hormones that are telling your body where to grow. Many of the important hormones that will help your body look more like a woman are actually made in fat cells. Without these fat cells, your hormones wouldn't be able to work properly.

Even though you may notice your body shape changing in different ways, not all of your weight is fat. Your muscles, bones, and body's organs are all growing and becoming heavier as well. Sometimes the weight part of your growth spurt happens before the height part and you may feel like you're growing out instead of up. *Don't worry, it's all going to come together and even out.* Expect to see differences in your body shape over the next three to four years. Things slow down after that and altogether, a girl may normally gain between 30–50 pounds by the time they reach 18.

Some girls don't like this change and feel like they are "getting fat." Often girls try not to eat anything to try to lose this new weight. This is the *worst* thing to do! Remember, your body needs a certain amount of fat in order for your hormones to work. Without this fat, you won't have enough hormones to complete your change into a woman. Many times professional gymnasts and ballerinas maintain such low body fat that they never reach their adult height and weight. They often don't develop completely because their hormones didn't have the body fat that was needed to work properly. This isn't so good because later on in life they could have brittle bones, no menstrual cycle and may maintain a more boyish figure.

You may notice that women that are the same height and weight often have different shapes. There are 3 basic body types. One type may be curvier around the hips and thinner around the waist. Another type may be tall and less curvy with smaller hips. A third type may look more muscular and be more balanced above and below the belly button.

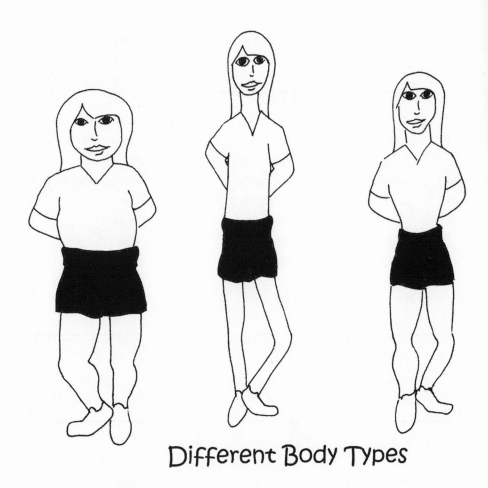

Different Body Types

Some women talk about being "big boned" and that's why they weigh more. Their body fat and muscles are just distributed in different places. We all have different body types that we inherit from our parents. Your actual weight in pounds is not important, it's the proportion between your height, your body fat and your body type that's important. Your doctor can tell you a good weight based on these things.

What is the perfect weight to be?

You may notice that many adults talk about being overweight or having too much body fat. This has nothing to do with the body changes that you are going through now. Adults have already gone through their height and weight spurts and need to maintain a healthy body which means lowering their body fat. Healthy doesn't mean being a certain clothes size but rather a weight that helps your body function at its best. This healthy weight will keep your heart strong and will help your other organs function so that you live a long and happy life. Weight is important but *healthy* is far more important to your body. The right weight to be varies from person to person. It is that weight which allows you to think, run, jump and do whatever you want to do without becoming too tired.

Should I eat more food during puberty to keep up with my growth spurt?

Instead of consuming empty foods like potato chips and candy, it would be better to keep up on the same healthy fruits and vegetables that fed your body as a child. Make sure to drink plenty of water (at least 6 glasses a day) and low fat milk (at least 2–3 glasses a day). Try to eat 3 different vegetables a day as well as a salad on most days of the week. A piece of fruit 2 or 3 times a day will keep you from being hungry and help you avoid junk food.

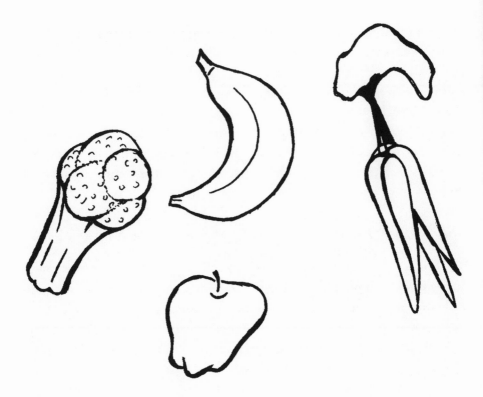

The best way to start out the day is eating breakfast. Healthy cereal, yogurt, fruit, and eggs are examples of nutritious foods that will fuel your body until lunch. Eating a good breakfast will give you the brain power to do well in school and the energy you'll need throughout the day.

Right now, your body is working at a rapid speed to do all the things necessary to grow into a woman. Once you are an adult, this body speed, also called your *metabolism*, slows down. Some women don't recognize this change in their metabolism and continue to eat as they did as a teenager. Extra food that your body doesn't need is then turned into excess fat tissue. This extra fat tissue can make it harder to exercise and may make you tired.

Adult commercials and magazine articles often advertise pills that promise to help you "lose weight." These rarely work and may even cause you to become ill. The *only* way to stay at a healthy weight is to eat properly and exercise every day. Ask any adult and they will agree with you;

unfortunately many adults are too busy to do the right thing for their bodies and become unhappy with extra unhealthy weight.

If I eat the right foods and exercise, will I look like the women I see on TV?

As a growing woman, you will see many examples of other women around you. In magazines, on television, and in movies you will see someone's idea of the "perfect women." They often have perfect hair, white teeth, no pimples, flat stomach, long legs, sometimes blonde hair, blue eyes and always very thin. Here's a secret-they really don't look like that.

Magazine pictures can be changed to make a woman's waist or legs look thinner. Movies are made with special lights around the actors to make them look more glamorous. Makeup is applied to the face and body to make them look a certain way, and contact lenses can change the colors of their eyes. Anyone can look like a movie star if they knew all of these tricks!

I bet that if you met your favorite movie star or rock star in person, you might find a pimple on her face or a little bit of fat around her hips or even fake hair. When she goes home from her job, she probably looks much like the rest of the women you see everyday in school, in the grocery store, or at the mall.

Why do so many women want to be skinny?

Many years ago, women tried to be as overweight as they could because this was a sign of being wealthy. As we learned about the human body and how to make it work better, we realized that too much body fat was not healthy and led to bad things like heart disease and cancer. Doctors told patients to keep their weight down and exercise more. Some women over-did it and became too skinny because they thought the skinnier you are, the healthier you are. So "skinny" became a sign of "healthy." This isn't exactly right because a girl can be thin and unhealthy at the same time if she doesn't eat the right foods.

Today, people now realize that skinny doesn't always equal healthy. The perfect woman eats the right foods to fuel her body and exercises to keep her heart strong, her brain healthy, and her muscles and bones in good condition. **The perfect woman isn't an image on a magazine cover; instead she is a confident woman who may have a thick waist or pimples on her face. She is happy with who she sees in the mirror and doesn't live up to someone else's expectations. Be confident with yourself and your body and *you* will be the perfect woman!**

Can you be TOO skinny?

As long as you are eating the right foods and exercising, being skinny is OK. But being too underweight can be as *unhealthy* as being overweight. If you are skipping meals or over-exercising to stay slim because you think it looks good then you're not treating your body well. Putting too much stress on your body will prevent it from developing properly and can cause health problems.

Underweight girls (like many fashion models and movie stars) can have heart problems, stomach problems, and catch more infections that make them sick more often. *Anorexia nervosa* is an eating disorder that makes a girl starve herself so that she can stay skinny. When she looks in the mirror she sees an overweight girl instead of who she really is. She may eat just tiny bits of food and exercise constantly.

Bulimia is another eating disorder that affects teens as well. In order to stay skinny, teens with this problem often will eat large quantities of food and then force themselves to vomit so that this food can't make them gain weight. Both of these disorders can lead to serious problems and even death. Fortunately, these girls can be helped. With the help of special counselors who are trained to deal with these problems, girls can get on the right track and start eating better and respecting their bodies.

BREAST CHANGES

"At first I didn't want to wear a bra because I thought everyone would notice."(Rosie, age 9)
"I was so flat-chested, I thought I would never develop." (Kate, age 16)
"I like wearing a bra, it makes me feel like a woman." (Leah, age 10)

For many girls, the first sign of puberty is the appearance of breasts. At some time during puberty you may notice small lumps developing under the nipple area on your chest. These are called *breast buds*. Breast buds are the very early stage of adult breast development. They can be quite painful at times but usually this discomfort resolves pretty quickly.

As your breasts start to enlarge and extend beyond your chest, you will notice that the dark area around the nipple also starts to separate and may become darker. This area is called the *areola* and may be dark brown, light brown, or pink. As your breast grows, your nipple will continue to point outward. If your nipple is *inverted*, it may point inward as your breast grows. This is very normal as well.

There are 5 stages of breast development. Some girls may start showing signs (like the growth of the areola and nipple) around age 7, while some won't start breast development until age 14! Usually, most girls start seeing changes in their breasts between 8 and 11 years old. Most girls have fully developed their breasts and reached the final stage 5 of development by 17 years old.

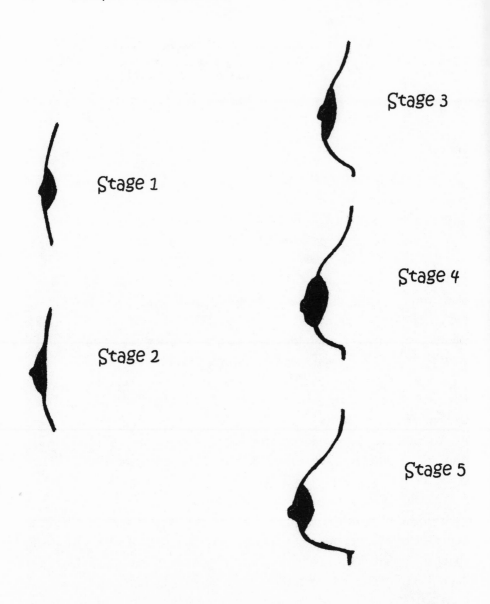

Stage 3

Stage 1

Stage 4

Stage 2

Stage 5

Stages of Breast Development

Help! My breasts are different sizes!

You may notice that both of your breasts are not exactly the same size. Most women's breasts are uneven. Because your breasts are rapidly growing inside, they can be very uneven at times. This usually evens out by the time you've completed puberty. Occasionally, one breast can be a full size different than the other. In this case, a bra can be used with an insert put into the smaller cup to even things up. If necessary, surgery can be done to correct a major difference once breast development has been completed. This is usually around 17 or 18 years old.

Why are my breasts itchy and sore?

Growing breasts can feel painful, itchy, swollen, or full. These are normal changes because of the rapid growth and increased blood flow to the breast tissue. This uncomfortable feeling usually goes away in a short time. If this becomes a major problem, a visit to the doctor might be needed so that he or she can prescribe a medicine to help you through this change.

Once you start your periods you might find that your breasts are very sore the week or so before you get your period. You can help relieve this tenderness by eliminating drinks with caffeine such as soda, coffee, and tea. Decreasing salty foods and chocolate can also help. Taking a mild pain reliever like ibuprofen or extra vitamin E can also help.

Will my breasts make milk when I go through puberty?

No. Your growing breasts are mainly made of fat tissue as well as tiny milk ducts. The milk ducts in your breasts are flat tubes that you really can't feel because of the surrounding fatty tissue protecting them. These tiny tubes all lead to the nipple and are responsible for making breast milk and delivering it to the nipple only when you are pregnant or nursing a baby. Even though you're not going to have a baby for a long time, your body is starting to prepare your breasts for when this happens.

When should I start wearing a bra?

This you get to decide for yourself. Some girls want to wear a bra because they are self-conscious about their changing breasts. Some girls start wearing a bra because they don't want their growing breasts to jiggle when they run. Some just want to wear a bra even if they haven't started into breast development. All of these reasons are OK.

There are so many kinds of bras, how do I decide?

Most girls start wearing a bra that looks like a very short undershirt. These are fine to wear but do not offer much support to growing breasts. Once your breasts start to develop and need a little more assistance you might want to look at bras that are a bit more fitted and offer more support.

Fitted bras come in different sizes. If you take a tape measure and measure around your rib cage right beneath your breasts, you will have a measurement in inches. Add 5 to this number and you will have your *band size*. The band size is usually a number between 28 and 44. The cup size is given in letters. The smallest cup size is AAA and the largest is EE. There are many ways to figure out your cup size, but it's probably best to try on a few different sizes to see which fits you the best.

Fitted bras come in many different styles. *Sports bras* are made of a material that absorbs sweat and may fit a little more snugly than other bras. This snug fit is meant to prevent the breasts from moving too much during exercise. If your breasts are not properly supported during any activity then they may become painful and sore. *Underwire* bras have a wire sewn into the seam to help support larger breasts. *Padded* bras have thicker cups to make breasts look larger. There are also bras called "*minimizers*" that help very large breasts look smaller.

Once you decide on the right bra size, don't be surprised if that size changes the next time you buy a bra. You may need to get a size larger or a different style as your body grows and reshapes. Puberty is one of many times you will notice changes in your breasts. You will notice changes when you gain or lose weight, especially during pregnancy. You may also notice some changes after breastfeeding. There are special bras made for each of these times.

The bottom line is always to try on each bra before you purchase it. The bra should fit so that you can move comfortably without your breasts bubbling out of the sides or top of the bra. Go ahead, jump around, lean over, do a jumping jack in the dressing room and make sure you've found the right one. Make sure the bra straps don't ride up in the back and that your breasts fit comfortably into the cup. If your breasts are bubbling over the sides or the bra feels too tight, try another one. Some bras are SO pretty but SO uncomfortable they will just sit in your drawer while others will feel so good you'll forget you're wearing one.

SKIN AND HAIR CHANGES

"My eyebrows are so much thicker than my younger sister's are."
(Danielle, age 10)
"My skin get so oily, I need to wash it much more than I used to."
(Alena, age 11)
"I had my first pimple on my cheek and boy was it painful!" (Grace, age 9)

While many girls can't wait to grow taller or develop breasts, most girls aren't as anxious to have their first pimple or get hair under their arms. Fortunately, there are ways to deal with some of these undesirable changes of puberty. There are many products available now that will help keep your skin looking healthy and your body well groomed. Facial soaps, acne medicines, shaving cream, and disposable razors are only a few of tools available to deal with your changing body.

What makes my skin so oily?

Your skin is made up of many tiny little pores. Some of these skin pores have a hair follicle growing out of it. Your pores are responsible for sweating, keeping your skin soft, and keeping you warm.

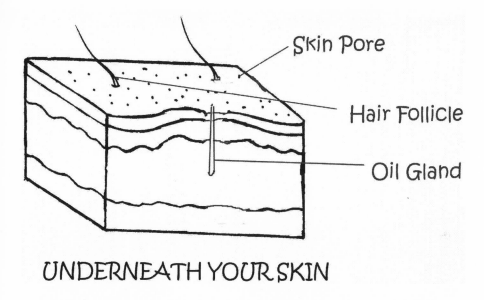

Skin Pore

Hair Follicle

Oil Gland

UNDERNEATH YOUR SKIN

During puberty, these pores start to secret more and more oil which is meant to keep the skin and scalp hair healthy. Your skin and hair may start to feel more oily and attract more dirt. It's important to remember to wash your face and hair more often during this time.

Will I be breaking out with pimples?

Some lucky girls never have a problem with breakouts. Most girls will have a few unwanted blemishes on their face before they've completed puberty. During puberty, your hormones not only make your skin more oily but make you sweat more. That leads us to the topic of *acne*. Acne is the medical term for what many teenagers call pimples or zits. Acne happens because as your pores start to secrete more oil and sweat, they can get clogged up with dirt and old sticky skin cells creating a plug in the pore. The buildup of oil pushes this plug to the surface. This is called a "black-head." When the skin bacteria irritate this plugged up pore it may appear as small white bumps or "whiteheads." As this irritation spreads to the surrounding skin, a painful pink or red pimple may form.

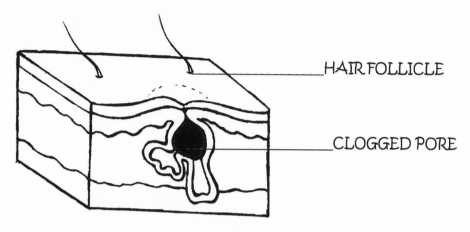

HAIR FOLLICLE

CLOGGED PORE

UNDERNEATH YOUR SKIN

In some girls, the skin on their face, chest or back may be affected with acne because of increased sweat and oil production in these areas. Washing you face with a facial cleanser or facial soap once or twice a day can help prevent the buildup of oil on your face. Bathing daily with a body soap that is "oil free" can help prevent acne from developing on your back or chest.

What can I do about my pimples?

There are many skin products to help treat acne. Some are very strong and may cause too much irritation and redness. One of the best products to use if you start "breaking out" with pimples is *benzoyl peroxide*. This cream helps decrease the bacteria that can cause pimples and helps unclog the plug blocking the pore. If you only have a few pimples you can use it only on that part of your face. If you have more severe acne then try using it in a thin layer all over your face.

If over the counter medicines don't help the situation, then doctors called *dermatologists* may be able to help. They may prescribe antibiotics and stronger creams to help clear up acne. **Try to resist the temptation to squeeze or "pop" a pimple because that will lead to scarring and make the area redder and more irritated.**

What can I do to prevent acne?

Many breakouts can be avoided. Drinking 6–8 glasses of water a day will help your skin and your whole body to keep your pores working right. Fruits and vegetables with plenty of vitamins will allow your skin to replenish and rebuild itself. Eating greasy foods like potato chips and cheeseburgers won't make your skin greasy but you may be contributing to acne by not eating the right foods.

To help prevent a visit from the Pimple Fairy, try to keep oily hair away from your face. Avoid using thick makeup on your skin which may clog up your pores even more. Keeping your fingernails clean and short will help prevent spreading bacteria and excess oil to your face and hair.

Stress is another big cause of acne. When you are stressed on the inside, your body has a way of showing it on the outside. You might try stress-relieving activities like listening to relaxing music and getting enough sleep. Exercising helps the blood flow to your skin and keeps it looking its best.

During puberty your hormone roller coaster is partly to blame for some breakouts; the changing hormones stimulate the skin pores to increase oil secretion. Pimples may only appear at certain times of the month like before your period. It's OK to wear cover up makeup that is *oil free* on these pimples so they don't seem to be so noticeable.

Will sunlight dry up my pimples?

No. Many girls think that lying in the sun will tan their face and help breakouts. This isn't true. The sun can actually *cause* more breakouts because of the harmful ultraviolet rays. Make sure to wear sunscreen made especially for faces during the warmer months. Don't forget to protect the rest of your body from the sun by using regular sunscreen during these months as well.

When should I start using deodorant?

As your body grows and matures you will sweat more. This sweat combines with bacteria found on your skin and creates an unpleasant body odor some call "B.O." Make sure to wash your body with soap everyday to decrease this odor causing bacteria. Always wear clean fresh clothes. Using an antiperspirant to decrease sweat and a deodorant to decrease odor will help keep you comfortable.

Combination antiperspirant/deodorant products come in many different forms. There are sprays, rolling balls that roll the liquid on, gels, and solid waxy-like blocks that you rub on. These should be applied under the arms after you bathe everyday. Try all different ones to see what feels good to you.

Because many deodorants contain perfume to make them smell good, you might find out that you get really itchy or tiny uncomfortable bumps under your arms after you use a certain product. This may be an *allergic reaction.* Just wash it off with some cool water and try a product that is "unscented" next time.

You really shouldn't need to use these products anywhere else other than your underarms if you bathe or shower everyday. If you have started shaving under your arms, be careful about applying deodorant immediately after shaving because it might create a burning sensation.

When should I start shaving?

You may notice that your body hair will also start to grow thicker and darker. It will become more noticeable on your legs, underarms, and around your *pubic areas (the area between your legs).* Hair on your chest, arms, and face may also grow thicker and darker. This is one of the first signs of puberty in many girls.

In some countries, the growth of this hair doesn't bother women and it is left alone. In this country, most women don't like this extra hair growth and consider removing it. There are many different ways of dealing with unwanted body hair. Most girls use shaving cream and razors but you can also use creams, waxes, and bleaches.

Many girls going through puberty want to start shaving their legs. *When* to start shaving your legs depends on the rules of your family and how responsible you are. Once you start shaving, you may need to keep up with it every few days depending on how fast your hair grows. If your leg hair is still fine and light colored then it's probably not noticeable and you shouldn't need to remove it. If it's starting to grow in thicker and you feel self-conscious about it, then perhaps it's a good time to consider removing it. Most girls start out by just shaving the thicker hair that grows between the knee and ankle. When the hair above the knee starts to become thicker, then consider shaving your whole leg.

What kind of razor should I use?

Most girls use disposable razors when they start shaving. They are discarded after a few uses. Reusable razors just discard the blade and attach a new blade to its handle. Disposable razors contain one, two, or even three blades. The more blades there are, the smoother your legs will feel after you shave but the more likely you are to cut yourself. Start out using just one blade until you feel more at ease with a razor and work up from there.

Electric razors are more expensive and have tiny permanent blades that are not as sharp as disposable razors. You can't cut yourself with an electric razor but it may not leave the skin as smooth after you're done shaving. There are also creams called depilatories that are applied to the skin and seem to dissolve away the hair without using a razor. These sometimes work well but may also cause an allergic reaction and irritate your skin.

What's the right way to shave?

There are a few important things that you should know before you start shaving. First you should properly prepare the skin by getting it wet for a few minutes. During this time you should apply a shaving gel or cream. This softens the skin and prepares it for easy hair removal by allowing the razor to glide smoothly over the skin. Don't use regular body soap because that may make the hair harder to shave and will dull the razor blade.

When you start shaving your legs, start from your ankle and go *against* the direction of hair. Use smooth, long strokes from your ankle to your knee. Keep a light touch on the razor; don't try to press it into your skin. **Be especially careful around bony areas such as the ankle or knee since the skin is thinner and may be easily cut.** If you do nick yourself, just apply some pressure with your finger or tissue and rinse it off. Small cuts will stop easily but larger cuts may need more pressure or a small bandage.

How about shaving other areas on my body?

A few years after you've started shaving your legs, you may want to move on to your underarms and "bikini line" which is the area where your upper legs and underwear meet. Usually hair growth here is less obvious and may not need to be shaven until you're well into your teen years.

The skin around these areas is very sensitive and easily irritated. Unlike shaving your legs, you should shave your underarms and bikini line by moving your razor in the *same* direction as the hair grows. Make sure to wet these areas and put shaving cream on for a few minutes before you shave. This will allow the skin to soften and prevent problems.

If care isn't taken while shaving these sensitive places, tiny red bumps can form a rash called "razor burn" and ingrown hairs can happen. Ingrown hairs occur when there is a small cut and the curly pubic hair grows back down into the skin causing a painful irritation. To avoid these problems, make sure to rinse the skin with cold water to close pores and prevent infection after you are done shaving. If you do get tiny red bumps you should try using 1% hydrocortisone cream on these areas to decrease the redness and swelling. You should always use a clean, fresh razor each time to prevent infection and unnecessary nicks and cuts. Never use an electric razor on your underarms or bikini line.

Most adult women shave their underarms, legs, and bikini line. Some girls get a little "shave crazy" and try to shave their arms, as well as the hair around their pubic areas. It won't make you sweat less or be any cleaner. Because your pubic hair is so thick, it will itch like crazy when it grows back which may last for a few weeks! A rash will most likely develop and you'll be very uncomfortable. Shaving these areas is definitely *not* necessary.

You may notice that some girls have unwanted hair that grows on their face, neck or arms. You should NOT remove this hair with a razor or cream before checking with an adult or a professional at a beauty salon. They can often help you decide on the best way to deal with this unwanted hair. Waxing to remove hair or bleaching to make it less noticeable are two options. Sometimes using medications to reduce this hair growth may also be necessary.

Do I have to shave?

American culture has set some basic guidelines that include shaving legs and underarms but it is ultimately your choice if you want to do it. Many girls choose not to shave and that's perfectly OK. Grooming is a personal choice and whether you decide to shave or not, you should always make sure that your body is clean, free of body odor, and neat in appearance.

GETTING YOUR PERIOD

"I feel so grown up" (Megan, age 11)
"You're kidding me, right? This is going to happen every month?" (Lisa, age 9)
"It really wasn't as weird as I thought it was going to be" (Caroline, age 16)
"So this is what all of the fuss is about?" (Tena, age 12)

Girls have such a wide range of reactions to getting their period. Some are happy, some are scared, some are worried, and some curious about what's really going on. These are all normal reactions. The secret to being prepared for your period is knowing exactly what's going on and what to expect. If you know what's going to happen when you get your monthly cycle, then you won't be frightened when it finally does happen-you might even feel relieved when it finally comes!

There are so many stories that have been passed down from mothers to daughters about their periods. Some women believe it cleanses you from the inside out (wrong). Some women believe you have built up toxins that need to be released (wrong). Many years ago, primitive people thought a woman having her period had the devil inside her (really wrong!). Many women know that the right reason; your period signals the end of a menstrual cycle. It means that the lining of the uterus that was preparing for pregnancy is no longer needed and is being released.

OK, so what's so cool about getting your period?

That's easy, your period is proof that your body has grown from a girl into a woman. It has passed nature's test and has shown you that your female parts are working just fine. You may not look any different on the day you get your first period but on the inside you're very different. Your body has matured and each month will continue to grow and prepare for the time when you may want to have a baby. Even though this won't happen for many years, your body needs time to grow and practice for this special event.

Your "period" is short for *menstrual period*. It means the few days each month when you will release a few tablespoons of bloody fluid from your vagina. This is called a *menstrual flow* because it trickles from your uterus, through your vagina, and out. Unlike the urine that comes from your bladder, you can't control your menstrual flow. That's why we have pads and tampons to absorb this fluid.

Where exactly is my uterus?

Most of the changes we have discussed so far are about changes happening on the *outside* of your body. Now let's talk about what's going on *inside* and review your female anatomy.

First, find your belly button (that's easy, huh?). Now go a few inches below your belly button and gently push down—it will feel soft and squishy. You are pushing down directly over your bladder and intestines. If you continue down in a straight line you will feel a hard bone which is your *pubic bone* which is covered with pubic hair. This bone is part of your pelvis. Your pelvis is a bony basket that holds and protects your *female organs*. Your female organs are your *uterus, two fallopian tubes, two ovaries* and a flattened tube called your *vagina*.

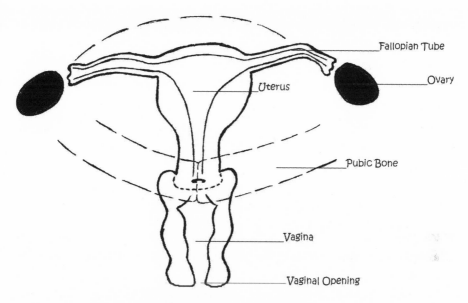

Your Inside Female Organs

Where does the menstrual blood come out?

If you keep marching down over your pubic bone, you will come upon your "*private area.*" We call it *private* because it's personal to you alone. If you ever feel irritated or think you're having a problem here then discuss it with an adult that you trust or your doctor. You should never have to show this area to family, friend or stranger in a way that makes you feel uncomfortable.

The openings to your internal female organs are found in this private area also called your *female genitals.* Outer lips covering this area are called the *vulva.* These fatty, hair covered lips protect the delicate areas inside the vagina. Many families have different names for your genital area. Some refer to it as "your privates," "your coochie", "your pee pee" or "down there." Your family may have another name as well. Knowing a little about your body's anatomy will make it easier to deal with your period.

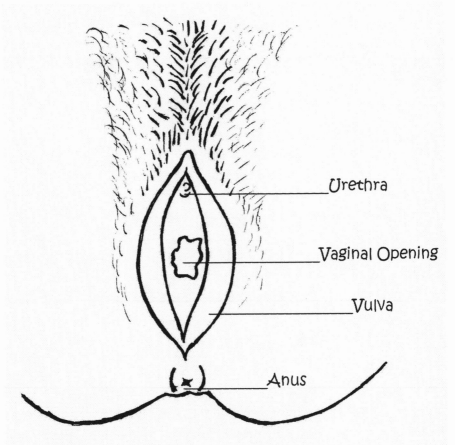

Urethra

Vaginal Opening

Vulva

Anus

Your External Female Genitals

Behind the lips of the vulva is your *vagina*. It is a flat tunnel that goes inward about 3–4 inches to your uterus. You won't be able to really see the vaginal tunnel because it's flattened, like a deflated long skinny balloon. This is where menstrual blood will flow out from your uterus when you start your menstrual flow.

If you can look at your vulva and vaginal opening with a mirror you will see your *urethra*. This is the opening where urine is released from your bladder and is located on top of the vagina. You will also see your *anus* under the vaginal opening. This is where your bowel movement comes out. In between those two places is the *vaginal opening.* This is the opening to your vagina. It may look like wrinkled pink skin but remember, it's flattened and only opens when needed, like when menstrual blood comes out or when you insert a tampon. If you're uncomfortable looking at your genital area, that's perfectly OK. You will find it easier to become more familiar with your body as you continue to develop.

I have a sticky discharge on my underwear, is this normal?

You may notice that your have a little dried discharge on your underwear now and then. This is a normal secretion that comes from the vagina when your body starts preparing for its menstrual cycle. It may be sticky, yellow, white, tan, or even slippery at times. If it gets to be too much or develops an odor, you may need to see a doctor to make sure you haven't developed an infection. Vaginal discharge is your body's way of keeping your vagina clean.

Do I need to use a douche?

A douche (pronounced *doosh)* is a bottle of water and/or vinegar that some women use to squirt water up into their vagina. You shouldn't need to wash inside your vagina or use a douche. Some women were taught to do this to clean out any discharge or menstrual blood. Just wash around the outside areas with soap and water. If you are irritated in this area, it may be from the perfumes in your soap or bubble bath. Try using *unscented* soap and plain bath water instead.

What causes your period to happen?

Your brain has been releasing hormones to help your body mature into a woman. As women, we have the unique ability to have babies. This process is very complicated and needs to be rehearsed many, many times before the time when we decide to have a baby. This rehearsal starts when we start our menstrual cycle. Most girls get their period around age 12 or

13. Some girls start as early as 8 or as late as 16-this all depends on your individual time clock.

Did you know that you were born with ovaries that contain all of the eggs that you'll ever need? Each month, one special egg (sometimes more) is selected to be the Egg of the Month. Since your ovaries are asleep for most of your childhood, the hormones of puberty are needed to wake them up so the contest can begin!

Ooh!Ooh! Pick me! Please, pick me!

Once your ovaries start to work, they also start to make hormones. These hormones will affect your whole body at different times during your cycle. As your ovaries are making these hormones, they also pop out a very small piece of jelly that contains this special Egg of the Month called an *ovum*. An ovum is as tiny as a drop of water and very soft and spongy. It may one day have the opportunity to make a baby. Since that won't happen for a long time, your ovaries practice releasing an egg every month so it will be ready when it's time.

Every month the Egg of the Month leaves the ovary and slides down the fallopian tube. During this time, you might feel some very small twinges of pain (that you'll probably think is gas!). This part of your cycle is called *ovulation* and usually happens about 2 weeks before you get your period each month.

As the ovary is picking the Egg of the Month, the uterus is busy preparing itself. It is making a nice thick spongy layer of tissue that will be ready to catch the ovum when it comes down the fallopian tube. Blood and other fluids continue to go to this spongy layer to prepare it. This layer that gets to be about as thick as a pencil is called your *endometrium*.

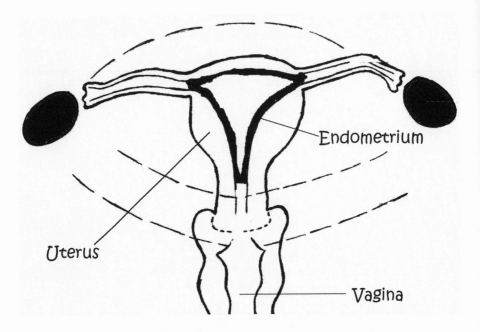

Your uterus is about the size of your fist. It is a muscle that is shaped like an upside down pear. Your fallopian tubes are attached on either side and they lead up to each of your ovaries. The endometrium lines the inside of your uterus. It will dissolve into a bloody fluid and become your menstrual flow when you start your period. The muscular walls of your uterus will help squeeze out this lining once it is signaled to by your ovaries.

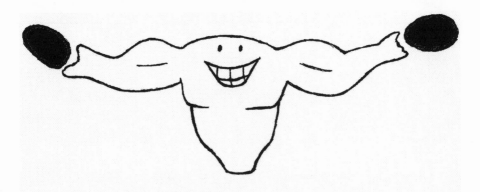

"I work hard so you don't have to!"

How will I know that all of this is happening?

For most of your menstrual cycle you'll be unaware of what's going on inside. Most of the things going on inside are painless. You may feel some small cramps or a little back pain. You may feel a little swollen around your lower abdomen before you see your period. You most likely will feel slightly stronger pains that are sharp and quick when you are actually starting your menstrual flow.

How much am I going to bleed?

The amount of menstrual flow can vary from just one tablespoon to 5 or 6 tablespoons. It may take just a few days for the endometrium to come out or last as long as a week. It may be bright red, dark maroon or even brown. All of this is normal. You may see pieces of tissue that look like skin with clumps of maroon blood or you might just see some spots. Again, this is all normal.

If you find that you are soaking through your sanitary pads every one hour or passing blood clots larger than a quarter you might want to mention it to a parent. This may happen during your first period but it shouldn't happen each time.

How often am I going to have my period? How long will it last?

You may get your first period and not have another one for several months. Once your body gets the hang of things, you should get a period about every 28–30 days. It usually lasts for 4–7 days and may be heavier on the first few days. It may last only 2–3 days or drag on for more than a week. If you have heavy bleeding that continues past a week or you are getting more than one period a month then you should check it out with your doctor.

By the time you finish your period, your ovaries and uterus gear up to start the whole process again. About 4 weeks from the first day of your period you might expect your next period. Many girls feel it's easier to keep track of your menstrual cycle by marking the first and last days of your menstrual flow on a calendar. This will help you remember to keep a pad and an extra pair of underwear in your backpack in case you need it. Some girls try to keep prepared by wearing a pad if she starts to feel cramps even if she hasn't started her menstrual flow.

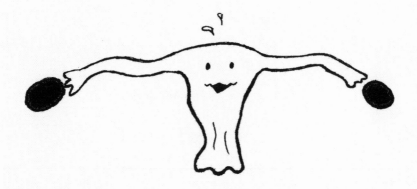

"Whew, I'm tired! I have to do this again next month?"

What is PMS?

You may find that your body and emotions change 7–10 days before you get your period. At times, you may feel like yelling or crying or both. Your mood may seem like it's on a roller coaster. You may be easily frustrated by little things and may not understand why you are feeling this way. Your body may feel swollen, tired or tender. These are all symptoms associated with PMS or *Premenstrual Syndrome*. They may seem worse right before your period. These symptoms pretty much disappear once you've started your menstrual flow.

Other PMS changes you may notice:

Cravings for salty or sweet foods	*Swelling in the lower belly*
Increased need to urinate	*Headaches*
Thirsty	*Frustration*
Belly pains or cramps	*Swelling in feet and hands*
Breast tenderness	*Diarrhea or constipation*
Crying for no reason	*Difficulty concentrating or making decisions*
Increased or decreased energy	*Pimples or acne*

You probably won't have all of these symptoms but may find that some will come and go with each period. You may feel like you just want to be left alone—this is OK. Your mind as well as your body may need to just chill out and rest. The best way to deal with PMS is to get a lot of sleep, eat healthy foods like fruit and vegetables, drink plenty of water, and continue to exercise. Soon your mood and body will change and life will be back to normal.

What can I do about menstrual cramps?

When your uterus starts to shed its lining, its muscle walls start to squeeze to help the flow leave the uterus. When this happens, you may feel some pains in your lower abdomen. These are menstrual cramps or uterine cramps. You may feel a dull, heavy feeling in your pelvic area. Sometimes, cramps feel like a sharp pain that comes and goes quickly. You may feel like you have to move your bowels or urinate.

A heating pad may help relieve some of this menstrual discomfort. There are many pain relievers made especially for menstrual pain such as ibuprofen, naproxen sodium, aspirin, or acetaminophen. If your cramps are so severe that over the counter medicines don't work, you may want to see your doctor for some other ways to deal with painful cramps.

Should I use pads or tampons?

You have a variety of options to protect your clothes from your menstrual flow. Sanitary napkins or "pads" are worn on the outside of your body. Tampons are inserted inside the vagina to absorb the menstrual flow. Both pads and tampons are made of a cottony like material that can absorb a lot of fluid. Most girls start out by using sanitary napkins when they get their period.

Sanitary napkins come in all shapes and sizes and are held in place by a sticky strip which attaches to your underwear. *Maxi pads* are thicker and longer and some are also available with wings that wrap around to further protect your underwear. Maxi pads are able to absorb alot of fluid and hold it within the pad so that it doesn't seep through and onto your clothes. *Mini pads* or *pantiliners* are thinner and absorb less fluid and are good to wear when your flow is not so heavy toward the end of your period.

Pads should be changed every 4 to 6 hours during the day, even if they aren't completely used up. This helps prevent an unpleasant odor from developing. You should also wear a pad (instead of a tampon) overnight. Since your flow will be lighter at this time, you shouldn't need to change it until the morning.

When you remove your pad, make sure to fold it up and wrap it completely in little bit of toilet tissue and throw it away in a trash can. *Never flush a pad down a toilet bowl, as it will most definitely clog up the plumbing.* Most of the pads sold today are disposable but some women may prefer reusable pads made out of cotton. These types of pads are cleaned by first soaking them in cold water and then washing them in a washer machine. Disposable pads are available at grocery stores and pharmacies and reusable pads are available at most health food stores and on the Internet.

Tampons are small, cone shaped cotton tubes that are inserted directly into the vagina to absorb the menstrual flow. *Tampons are okay to use at any age and can be used during your first period if you want to.* Inserting tampons requires a little more practice than using pads but they allow you greater flexibility in the activities that you can do while you are on your period, like swimming.

Tampons come in different sizes and also vary in how much menstrual fluid they can absorb. There are junior tampons made for younger women to super plus tampons made for women with heavier flows. Tampons also vary by the type of applicator they use. Some have a plastic applicator, which may slide more easily into the vagina, some have a cardboard applicator, and some tampons come without an applicator at all.

Inserting a tampon may seem like a scary and confusing task. Most girls can easily learn to do it. You may want to ask your mother or other close female relative to help you if you have a problem. If you feel embarrassed about asking for help with such a personal thing just try another time when you're a little more relaxed.

How do I put in a tampon?

OK, as nervous as you might be, try to relax. You can definitely do this. First, put your foot up on a toilet bowl or small stool. Look at your vaginal opening with a hand mirror. You may need to separate the small lips of the vulva to locate the vaginal opening. Hold the tampon with the pointer finger over the plunger and your thumb and middle finger over the ribbed rim in the middle of the applicator.

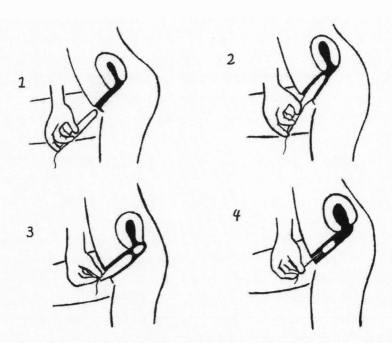

How to Insert (1,2,3) and Remove (4) a Tampon

Now, place the tip of the tampon applicator against the vaginal opening (Figure 1) and slowly insert or slide the applicator(which already has the tampon in it) into the vagina while aiming toward the lower part of your back. Once you've inserted the tampon into the vagina all the way until the ribbed rim (the fingers holding the applicator should be touching the vaginal opening), slowly push the inner tube which will push the tampon into the vagina (Figure 2). If it seems too difficult to plunge the tampon then pull the applicator out a little bit and try again to push the plunger in while keeping the first part of the applicator still.

Don't worry; you can't push the tampon into the wrong place. Imagine the vagina is a short sock and you're pushing the tampon into the end of the sock. Once you have completely plunged the inner tube into the applicator, remove both tubes together by sliding them out over the string until completely removed (Figure 3).

The first time you insert a tampon you may feel like it's not in the right position. Go sit down and relax, if it's still uncomfortable you can try gently pushing it in a little bit more (without the applicator) until it feels more comfortable. If it is still uncomfortable you probably didn't insert it far enough in past the muscles of the opening of the vagina. If still not right, just gently pull the string and remove the tampon and discard it (Figure 4). Try again in a few hours. Most tampons are flushable but the applicators are not. These need to be wrapped in toilet tissue and placed in a trashcan. If a tampon is properly inserted, you shouldn't feel it at all after a few minutes.

So many times, first time tampon users tense up so much that they tense up their vaginal muscles making it very difficult to insert a tampon. Try not to bear down while you're inserting it or consider inserting it while sitting on a toilet seat instead. The most important thing to remember about inserting and removing tampons is to *relax*. If your vagina feels too dry you might try to use a lubricating jelly to help with the insertion. Lubricating jelly can be purchased at any pharmacy and are located by the vaginal products.

If it just seems too uncomfortable, put it away and try another time. You *will* be able to do it. If you really need some help you can ask your mother or close female friend. You can also visit with a gynecologist who will teach you the proper way to insert a tampon comfortably.

I've never met a woman who couldn't use a tampon if she wanted to. I've met plenty of women who *thought* they couldn't use a tampon. This was probably because they were too tensed up when they tried to insert one or the tampon was not the right size for them. They may have never tried one because they were told by their parents that using a tampon can hurt you.

Luckily for you, tampons now come in so many sizes that there is definitely one that will be comfortable for you. Make sure to buy "slim" tampons and read the directions in the box that are specifically for that brand. Once you're more comfortable with inserting and removing tampons then move onto the regular size and absorbency. Avoid deodorant tampons for now because they may cause an allergic reaction.

Make sure you change your tampons every 4–6 hours and sooner if they feel heavy or uncomfortable. You may also want to wear a small pad along with your tampon to make sure you don't leak through your underwear.

What is Toxic Shock Syndrome?

Toxic Shock Syndrome (TSS) is an infection that can happen if harmful bacteria are allowed to develop in the tampon. Symptoms of TSS are high fever, vomiting, and diarrhea. There can also be a headache, sore throat, and a peeling red rash that looks like sunburn. If these symptoms should develop you should immediately remove the tampon and see a doctor. Toxic Shock Syndrome is very rare and can be avoided if you change your tampon regularly.

What if I can't find my tampon?

First locate the string between the lips of the vagina and slowly pull the tampon out of the vagina. Occasionally, the string may be coiled up between the lips of the vagina and can be brought down. If you can't find it, just bear down and grasp the end of the tampon with your thumb and pointer finger and remove it that way. If you forget you have a tampon in for a longer period of time, simply remove it when you remember. There may be a foul odor in the vaginal area for a day or so. If it doesn't go away you may want to see a doctor.

Do I need to remove a tampon if I need to urinate?

Tampons do not need to be removed when you urinate or have a bowel movement. The tampon is in your vagina, which is a separate opening from where urine and stool come out. If the tampon string gets wet, you can wipe it with toilet paper or a tissue. Once a tampon is properly placed in the vagina it can't fall out so don't worry.

Should I use a tampon when I'm not on my period?

You shouldn't need to use a tampon when you are not having a period. Your regular light vaginal discharge is meant to cleanse your vagina and shouldn't be absorbed by a tampon. It's okay to wear a light mini pad when you are not having your menstrual period. If your vaginal discharge becomes heavy or foul smelling, you may want to check it out with a doctor.

Are tampons safe to use for everybody?

Tampons are very safe. Some women may be uncomfortable with using tampons, probably because they were told they weren't healthy. Some women believe that a tampon can make it difficult for you do have a baby when you're older or can cause medical problems. All of these myths are wrong. When used correctly, tampons are a safe alternative to using sanitary napkins and will enable a girl to feel more at ease and allow her to do anything she wants to do while having her period. It's your choice. You should use what you feel comfortable with.

Will everyone know when I am having my period?

Getting your period is one of most important and final changes that you will experience during puberty. Your family and friends may notice how tall you've gotten or may remark about your changing figure. Even though your uterus and ovaries are hard at work during your menstrual cycle, your period is personal to you. Your friends and family won't know you're menstruating unless you tell them. You will need to take extra special care of yourself during your menstrual period and be a little more prepared for unexpected bleeding. If you need help, just ask your school nurse, parent or another female. They've all been through it! Getting your period is a very special time and is your initiation into the biggest club around-womanhood.

Just as a beautiful flower grows from just a seed into a beautiful blossom, so will you. You will make the miraculous transformation from a girl into a woman. Your mind and body will continue to grow and accept all of the new challenges that await you. Becoming a woman isn't easy, but if you understand the changes that your body is undergoing, you'll handle everything just fine.

Remember to accept these changes and always try to understand why they are happening. Don't be upset if you get a pimple or a period cramp. Try to keep the whole picture in mind and understand that becoming a woman is a very special and complicated process that will allow your body to do so many wonderful things.

Good luck and congratulations!

978-0-595-34220-4
0-595-34220-5